AN EYEWITNESS BOOK

688.72

20254

# Toys in History

## ANGELA SCHOFIELD

WAYLAND PUBLISHERS

# More Eyewitness Books

First published 1978
SBN 85340 453 4
Copyright © 1978 by Wayland (Publishers) Ltd
49 Lansdowne Place, Hove, East Sussex BN3 1HF
Text set in 14pt Photon Univers printed by Photolithography, and
bound in Great Britain at The Pitman Press, Bath

# About this book

Toys are as old as mankind itself. Even cavechildren had toys to play with and many of today's most popular playthings go back to early times. Hobby horses, for example, were enjoyed by children in the Middle Ages and before. The amazing talking and walking dolls in the wonderland of today's toyshops are not really new. More than a hundred years ago discs were fitted into dolls' bodies to make them recite rhymes.

The pictures in this book show you children's toys and games through the ages in many lands. There is a chapter on modern toys to tempt you, too!

Some of the words printed in *italics* may be new to you. You can look them up in the word list on page 92.

# Contents

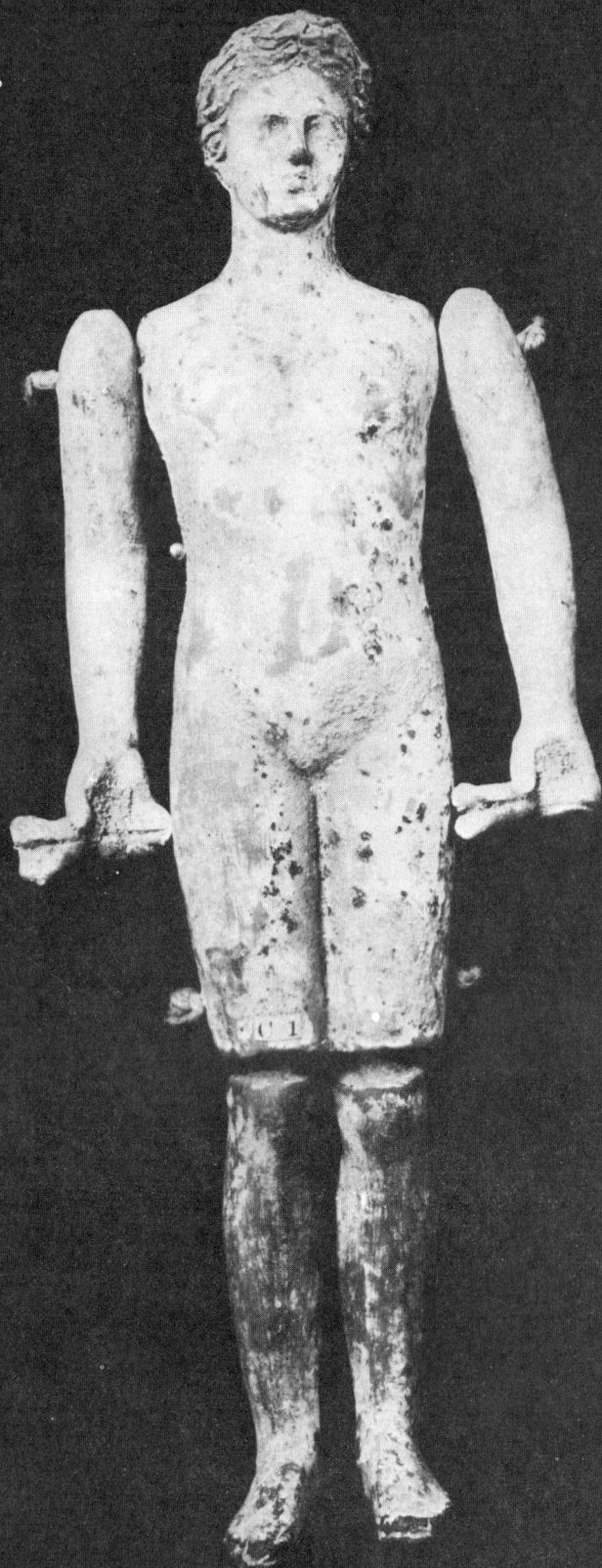

# 1. The Earliest Playthings

From the beginning of time, babies and young children have been amused or soothed by bright and interesting objects. Some of these playthings were early versions of toys we know today. Thousands of years ago, cavechildren had balls which rolled and bounced. They made them from dried fruit or even the bladders of animals. Sometimes dried fruit with seeds in would make rattles. Any bundle of rags or fur could become a "doll". So could a piece of plain wood, if it was wrapped up.

Not all early toys were as simple as that. Three thousand years ago, children in Persia (we call it Iran now) pulled along toy animals on wheels. You can see a toy clay boat, complete with oarsmen, in Hull Museum. It was made in the Bronze Age, nearly four thousand years ago. The ancient Egyptians made clay dolls with arms and legs that could be moved. Some of these dolls have been found in tombs. The doll in the picture is Greek.

Two toys that are popular today were used very differently long ago. Kites helped the Chinese to measure distance over two thousand years ago. And would you believe that yo-yos were once weapons in the Far East?

Children in ancient times had educational toys, too. Boys practised with miniature bows and arrows so that they could be hunters when they grew up. And girls were given small spindles to train them to be housewives.

A BONE TOY   This little Stone Age girl seems to be playing with a bone. Perhaps it's her doll. She could amuse herself outside the cave where she lived, playing with pebbles, sand, mud, snow, and other natural things she found. Anything round could be used as a ball. A beautiful little clay house on stilts was found in Europe dating from *Neolithic* times, and perhaps some child of ancient times played dolls' houses with it.

**FLYING CHINESE DRAGONS** The Chinese enjoyed interesting toys centuries before children in our country. Fascinating kites in dragon designs are recorded in 206 BC for measuring distances as well as to amuse the flyer. Another Chinese paper toy was a ball, made of tightly-screwed paper tied with string. The Chinese believed that rattles kept away evil spirits. And the funny round doll which bounced back when knocked over was supposed to remind children of the Buddhist monk whose legs withered away while he meditated for nine years!

GREEK SPORTING TOYS   Most ancient Greek toys were meant to make children take exercise and grow stronger. A sort of hobby horse is mentioned by Socrates, the Greek writer, and there are many pictures and statues of children playing with hoops.

Pictures on Greek vases show children pulling little carts with wheels. Toy chariots and carved war horses were also popular. Soft skin balls stuffed with wool were baby toys, but a singing bird whistle, filled with water to make a warbling sound, must have amused everyone!

EGYPTIAN DOLL'S CRADLE Small objects discovered in Egyptian tombs are not always toys. Often miniatures of everyday items were buried to help the dead in the next world! But Egyptian children had balls to play with, made of plaited *papyrus*, as well as tops and carved animals. A wooden tiger with an opening jaw showing sharp bronze teeth was made about 1000 BC. Little pottery animals have been found, too. Sailing toy boats was another popular pastime.

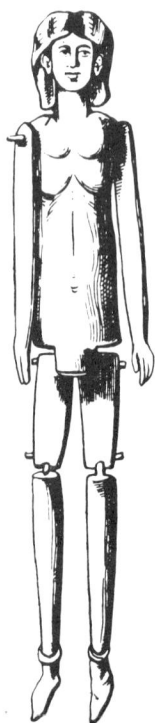

A ROMAN REWARD  The Greek girls are playing knuckle bones or fivestones — a very ancient game you have probably seen. In Roman times, children were given knuckle bones as a reward for good conduct. Young children had clay rattles baked into pig or bird shapes. In a museum at *Hadrian's Wall* you can see a set of tiny clay plates and cups made when Britain was under Roman rule. Little girls loved their jointed dolls. Plutarch, the Roman writer, says that his two-year-old daughter wanted her nurse to give her doll some milk too!

VIKING WARRIORS  These magnificent chessmen are believed to be Viking. They were discovered in the Hebrides. Other table games, such as dice and chequers, were played at this time. Clay dolls which rattle have been discovered in Viking burials. We are not certain whether these are actually toys, or whether they had some religious significance in the burial ceremony.

BABY BATTLE AXES   This little Saxon girl has a live toy to play with, but generally childhood was not much fun in those days. Education in a monastery could begin as early as three years old. Tiny battle axes and farming tools suggest that children were prepared for adult work. But chessmen and draughts have been found and exciting stories of monsters and giants entertained adults and children alike.

TOY NORMAN KNIGHTS   No wonder these boys have chosen swordsmen as their puppets. It must have been exciting to play swordfights with these puppets, jerking their lead feet with strings! No doubt the fathers of these boys were soldiers themselves. Boys also liked models of horses and wooden carts. We read of girls' dolls in Norman times, but unfortunately none of these survive today. Hobby horses were probably introduced into Britain by the Normans.

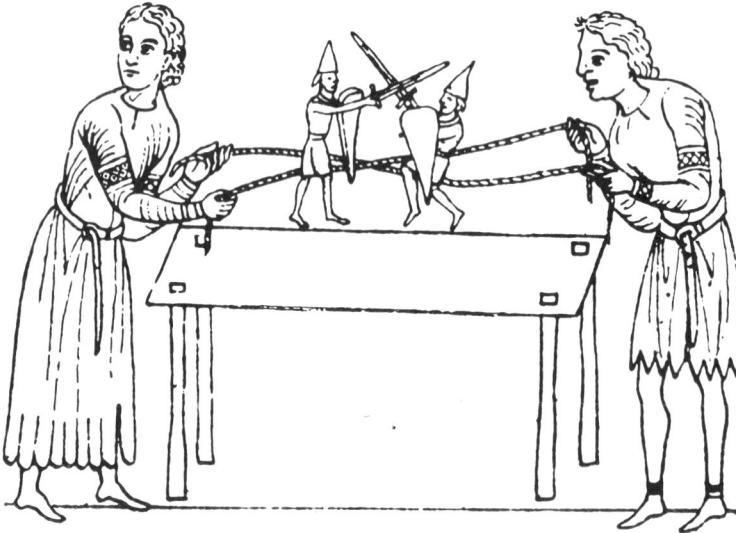

16

# 2. The Middle Ages and after

As we have seen, there is little known about toys in this country until about the eleventh century, when the Normans brought their warlike toy soldiers and horses.

There were certainly toymakers at the beginning of the *Middle Ages*, but very few actual toys have survived. This is not surprising. Toys were made of wood, rag or even paper, and in those cruel times the burning of villages was quite common. The earliest toys found are made of clay. They include dolls, soldiers, horses and knights, and tiny kitchen tools and furniture. Shopkeepers and toymakers sold their toys at markets and fairs, such as the St Bartholomew's Day Fair held every year in London on 24th August. *Medieval* pictures show children playing with balls, windmills and puppets. But toys were not only for children. You can see how the grown-ups are joining in the play in this picture, even though it is called "Children's Games". It was painted by the Flemish artist Pieter Breughel in 1560.

In the sixteenth and seventeenth centuries great progress was made in the making of toys, and the ways in which they were sold. Children played with toys far away from the places where they were made. The early American explorers used toys, es-pecially dolls, as well as other interesting objects, to *barter* with the native Indians. In Europe, German toys were famous. And so began the spread of a variety of playthings all over the world.

SOLDIERS AND HORSES *Archaeologists* in Strasbourg, France, have found clay models of fourteenth-century horsemen. In Paris, tin and lead soldiers a hundred years older were discovered when the River Seine was dredged. These were

probably sold from little shops on the river bridges. The popularity of horses as toys shows the importance of the horse in everyday life at this time. Boys were trained as knights from the age of seven, so it is not surprising that their toys were rather warlike!

HOBBY HORSES AND LANCES   The prancing horse in this picture is a version of the ancient toy known throughout history. Made simply with a stick and a model horse's head, you could make one today with a broom handle and an old stuffed sock! You could even add a wheel and rope reins. Another boy is carrying a kind of whirling windmill. These were also used as toy *jousting* lances, intended to knock your opponent off his hobby horse.

A PUPPET SHOW    Puppets are among the
earliest toys. Manuscripts from the fourteenth century show children watching puppet shows, given in
little *booths* just like Punch and Judy shows today.
In 1661 the Duchess of Suffolk paid six shillings
and sixpence to "two men who played upon puppets".
This would have been a very high wage at the time.
A year later Samuel Pepys wrote in his famous
*Diary* that he saw the first Punch and Judy show in
London. So many puppeteers were foreign that
often a director stood in front of the stage to explain
the story.

DICE  "I wish to warn you against dice and betting
        Gambling's the very Mother of robbed purses. . . ."

So ran the advice of the poet Geoffrey Chaucer in the fourteenth century. Playing with dice and betting were as common then as when the Roman soldiers played at dice for Christ's robe. These simple cubes of bone with their pattern of dots (seen being made in the picture) ruined many a fortune and even cost lives.

BOBBING FOR APPLES  These young men are having fun trying to catch an apple which is dangling on a string. Perhaps you play a game like this at Hallowe'en? The idea is to try to take a bite out of the apple without touching it with your hands. It's very difficult! Try it if you haven't already.

PLAYING BOWLS   This brother and sister are playing bowls in the garden. Bowls is just one of the many games which can be played with balls. It was popular over a long period. There is a story that Sir Francis Drake, the sea captain, was still playing bowls at Plymouth when the Spanish Armada appeared in 1588. Obviously he finished his game in time to save England from invasion!

Destmics a althalenta
ar plus que top tint faset

HOCKEY AND TENNIS These students are playing a rough kind of hockey in the street. Hockey is a
very ancient game, and we know that it was played
in England as early as 1277. In Shakespeare's famous
play *Henry V,* the young King's enemy sends him a
barrel of tennis balls. The joke misfires when Henry
proves he's as good at war as he is at tennis! The two
young men playing club ball use strong pieces of
wood to hit the ball to each other (below).

CUP AND BALL    This game took France by storm
in the sixteenth century and soon spread to other
parts of Europe. The simplest version consisted of
a small wooden ball attached by a piece of string
to a cup. But it was quite difficult to catch the ball in

La foire franche
des Bilboquets
de plus à lamode

the cup. It was not just a children's toy. Many grown-ups joined in the craze, especially when the cup was replaced by a small peg to make it even more tricky. Sometimes it was known by its French name "bilboquet".

**LEARNING TO READ** From an early age, rich children were encouraged to read, sometimes in more than one language. Alphabet bricks date from the time of Elizabeth I. This is how children's books were made in those days—first take a piece of wood with a short handle. On to this place a sheet of parchment with the letters of the alphabet. Then cover it with a piece of transparent animal horn to protect the parchment from the child's pointer!

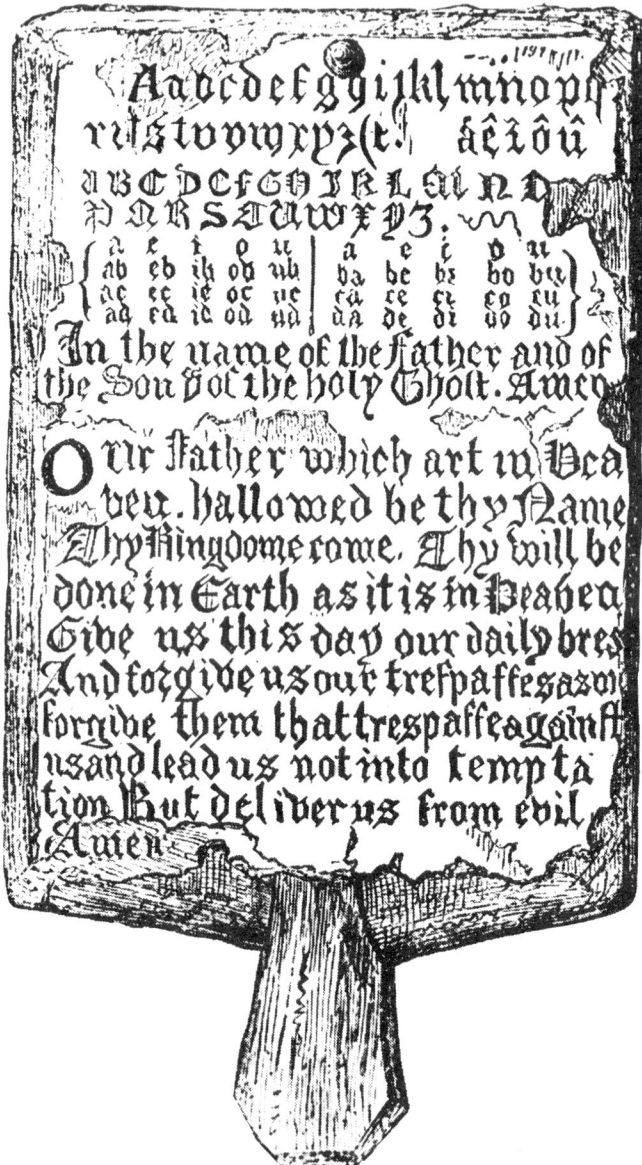

A CORAL RATTLE   This little girl's rattle is made of coral from the sea and carved into the shape of a wolf's tooth. With its jingling bells it was a toy to amuse her and perhaps her dog, too! But the smooth shape would also make it suitable for a baby to bite on. In ancient times, people believed that rattles had magic powers to keep away evil spirits, and that coral was good for the eyes. Coral rattles like this one were usually made in France.

LADY ARABELLA'S DOLL   Lady Arabella Stuart's doll is dressed in stiff, uncomfortable clothes like her own. It was probably made of wood and leather, and stuffed with bran. Cheaper dolls were made of cloth. Some dolls were hollow, for filling with coins or sweets as gifts. Dolls made in Germany had moveable arms and legs. Simple Dutch dolls with painted hair and jointed arms and legs were popular too. Sometimes they were called "Flanders babies" or "penny woods". There was a rhyme at the time:

"The children of England take pleasure in breaking What the children of Holland take pleasure in making."

ROYAL ROCKING HORSE This strange old rocking horse once belonged to King Charles I. It was made of wood with a padded leather seat or "saddle". No doubt he played all kinds of make-believe games on it before mounting a live horse. Children in America especially enjoyed rocking horses in the early days.

BOYS' TOYS The small picture shows the toys boys played with long ago. You probably recognize and play with them too! There are balls, stilts, a whipping top and a kind of skittles. One boy has made a swing on a tree, just as you can today with an old tyre. Perhaps you would like to play with the miniature crossbow! The marbles would probably have been made of stone or clay and possibly came from Holland.

34

# 3.  Eighteenth-Century Toys

As we have seen, most early toys were not specially made for children to play with. This began to change in the eighteenth century, when grown-ups realized that children were not just small adults. Now they started making toys that would teach children, and toys that would amuse lively young people with lots of imagination.

It was a time when machines were invented to do marvellous things. Many of the toys were mechanical, too. Dolls and carriages could move by clockwork when they were wound up. But as always, such expensive and elaborate toys were only for the children of the rich. Most poor children went to work and had little time for play. However, cheap toys made of tin and lead became popular. They were sold in the first real toyshops.

This does not mean that children stopped playing with familiar toys. They still liked tops, hoops and balls. Some toys were made even better. The hobby horse became a clumsy sort of rocking horse, and famous architects and cabinet makers built the very best dolls' houses. Books were written for children, too. And many alphabet rhymes and nursery rhymes come from this period.

Unfortunately, few toys made in the 1700s survive today. Children must have played with them until the toys fell to pieces and had to be thrown away!

PAPER TOYS   Paper was used as a simple and cheap material for toys. Flat paper cut-out dolls with clothes were as popular two hundred years ago as they are today. Clothes were cut out and painted, then fitted over the shoulders with tabs. There was also a paper toy called a "pantin" which was loosely jointed and jerked by strings—half-way between a doll and a puppet. It was enjoyed by adults and children alike.

WHO BUILT THE ARK?   The earliest Noah's arks were made in the seventeenth century, when the careful carving of as many as two hundred pairs of animals made them expensive. It is thought that arks were made originally in Oberammergau in Germany, where they were carved alongside toy farms with similar animals. By the eighteenth century the work of carving toy arks was divided among a number of workers. This made them cheaper and so more children could own them.

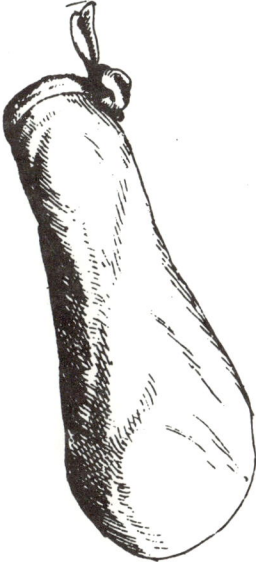

**BABY HOUSES** A popular entertainment at travelling fairs in earlier times was the peep show. This was a box with stand-up paper figures. The eighteenth century improved on the idea with "baby houses". They were not really toys. Young ladies

enjoyed them most. They collected finely-detailed miniature furniture for these box-like houses. So fierce did competition become, that often famous architects and cabinet-makers were called upon to make and furnish them.

VISUAL TOYS   In 1785, an Edinburgh painter called Robert Barker showed spectators a strip of painted scenery gradually unfolding around them. He called this his "panorama". It was one of the many moving entertainments of the century. Soon small toy panoramas were made, often showing the funeral of the Duke of Wellington! A simpler toy called a "thaumatrope" consisted of a disc twirled on a string so that the pictures on each side merged and, for example, a bird appeared inside a cage!

**WALKING DOLLS**   Early moving dolls sometimes walked by clockwork when wound up. Others moved on wheels. There was even one which could waddle down a slope while pushing a cart! Originally, dolls were made to dance on *harpsichords* when the vibrations set up by the instruments caused bristles beneath their skirts to move!

**PRAMS AND CRADLES**   This comfortable-looking pram is taking a toddler for a ride. Smaller versions were used for dolls. Carved wooden rocking cradles, just like a baby's but smaller, were popular with little girls from the time of Queen Elizabeth. The young lady in the doorway seems to be enjoying the children's swing! (Opposite.)

**A POUPARD**   Another puppet-like toy which was popular towards the end of the period is called a "poupard". It looks like Mister Punch and has jingling bells and a musical movement which plays when the stick is twisted. Children also enjoyed hand puppets and *marionettes*. The famous characters of the Italian puppet plays—Harlequin and Columbine—come from this time. So does the jack-in-the-box. It works when a tight spring is released as the box is opened.

Heb. 12:22.    Rev. 2:7

Country of

**BEU** Enchanted **LAH**
Out of Giant Despair's coach
Hopeful    Ground is drawn    Here ... & Elijah went up

They are caught in a nett Prov. 29:5
They are ... kept and sent away
They are Turnaway

Broadway Gate Matt. 7:13

Dead Mans Lane

Conceit

Mount Error 1 Tim 2:17,18

Mount Clear
Mount Caution

Emanuel Land

A byeway to Hell here
Vain Confidence fell into this Pit

By Path Meadow

Christian & Hopeful Erect a Pillar

River of the Water of Life

Good Confidence

Doubting Castle

Lots Wife

A Beautiful Meadow Psal. 22

Great Grace lived here

Hill Lucre A Silver Mine

Demas 2 Tim 4:10

Little faith lived here

Sincere

Love-gain

At Vanity Fair Faithful was burnt & Christian met Hopeful

Vanity Fair

Honesty

County of Coveting

Evangelist

They are Pliable

Fair speech

Dark Mountains

Gracelefs

Valley of the Shadow of Death

A large Wood

Vain Glory

Formality & Hypocrisy came from hence

Apollyon

House Beautiful

Hill Difficulty

The way called Danger

Formality & Hypocrisy tumble over the Hill

Simple, Sloth, Presumption are asleep

Mount Sinai

Morality

Hee Christian

kept his burden ... expects Jesus

Beelzebubs Castle

Wicket Gate Luke 13:24

Evangelist meets Christian again

Apostacy

Help pulls him out

Slough of Despond

Pliable turns back

City of Destruction

Carnal Policy

**THE FIRST JIGSAW** The world's first jigsaw was made in the 1760s when John Spilsbury, a teacher at Harrow School, cut up a map of the British Isles. He gave the pieces to his pupils and asked them to remake the map correctly. At first jigsaws were meant to make geography and history more interesting. They were called dissected puzzles and they did not interlock. It was not until the early 1900s that a fretsaw was used to cut the pieces into zig-zag shapes. Then they were called jigsaws, zagsaws and zig zags.

MUSICAL PASTIMES The Graham children in this painting by William Hogarth are being entertained by the boy's musical box. But the cat seems more interested in the frightened cheeps of the

caged bird! As he turns the handle, the boy makes a tinkling tune to amuse his sisters. There is also a pull-along bird which flaps its wings as the wheels go round.

FAMILIAR GAMES   Here are some familiar
games which were enjoyed by children in the
eighteenth century. Many are still played today.
Badminton certainly looks easier to play without a
net! The kite in the picture looks very much as it
must have done over the centuries. The hoop and
whipping-top continued their popularity well into
the 1900s.

MORE GAMES Young people in eighteenth-century England liked playing with a feathered shuttlecock and a heavy racket called a battledore. The idea was to hit the shuttlecock over a net to an opponent, rather like badminton. The young men are blowing balls with pipes, rather like our "blow football". Another popular game was blowing darts at a numbered board. This was called "blowpoint".

# 4. The Victorian Nursery

"Dear Santa Claus, I would like a desk and chair, a box of chokolate, a dolls wardrobe and an *ocarina* Signed Anne Garlick 1884."

This letter was discovered in the chimney of a house in Derbyshire nearly a hundred years after young Anne wrote her request for toys typical of the Victorian nursery. We must imagine a time of childhood different from today. Children, remember, were "seen and not heard", and their toys kept them quiet and out of the way of adults. Nannies were employed in all but the poorest families. The elaborate toys we shall examine belonged to the richer children. But a touching example of a poor child's toy is displayed in Edinburgh's Museum of Childhood—a doll made from an old shoe, wrapped in rags and with a face carved in the heel. Contrast this with the exquisite dolls—but remember it was probably all the more appreciated, as the child made it herself.

The nineteenth century saw enormous steps forward in trade, inventions and knowledge. Now, very complicated mechanical toys were made. New entertainments such as the magic lantern came on the scene. Scientific toys became popular, and all the practical games through which Victorian children were expected to learn basic facts of history, geography, mathematics and scripture. Exciting new wheeled toys, especially trains, became popular with the opening of the first railways, and in 1851 the Great Exhibition in London showed a dazzling collection of mechanical dolls and toys.

SEEN AND NOT HEARD In many Victorian homes, only the quietest of activities were allowed on Sundays. Very little work was done in the house and the children were allowed to play only with special Sunday toys. These were instructive, usually with a Biblical background. There were puzzles;

cards with questions and answers; or a Noah's ark. Another quiet activity was building with toy blocks. There were several kinds, made of wood or stone, and shaped in cubes, blocks, arches and pillars. Some had alphabet letters. Others were arranged in different patterns or shapes to make pictures.

SCRAPS AND SCREENS   The cosy atmosphere of the Victorian nursery was helped by a scrap screen. It shielded chilly children from windy chimneys and badly-fitting doors. Children could buy cut-outs to stick on screens. The decorated screens were then varnished. Cut-outs could be collected and swapped, and pasted on trays and in scrapbooks. This pastime is not so popular now, but perhaps you have a scrapbook for pictures cut from magazines. Pressing and mounting flowers was another rainy-day amusement for Victorian children.

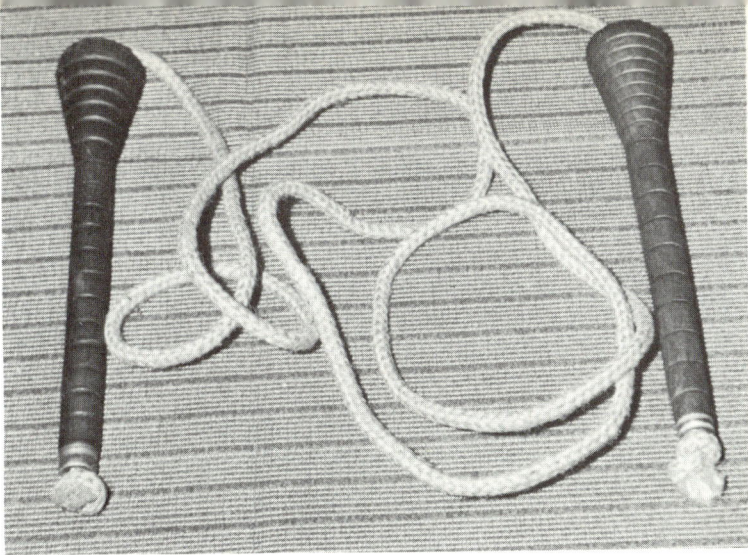

SALT, MUSTARD, VINEGAR    Children could be just as active and noisy in the nineteenth century as their descendants in the twentieth. Look at these old skipping ropes. The picture above shows that the handles are weaving *bobbins*! Once these were used in the cotton mills of northern England. Children must have begged the old worn-out ones from the mill foremen and tied them to an old piece of window *sash cord*. Windows in those days slid up and down on ropes.

**MUSICAL TOYS** Victorian children had a wide choice of noisy musical toys to play, apart from the comb and paper mentioned in one of Robert Louis Stevenson's poems! Anne Garlick's *ocarina* was a small egg-shaped china instrument blown to produce a note. Of course there were trumpets, whistles and drums, as well as small versions of other musical instruments. Not for Sundays, though!

**COME WITH A HOOP** "Come with a hoop, come with a ball" says the nursery rhyme. Certainly hoops were still popular in Victorian times. They were simple and cheap. The outer rim of a barrel would do, so that even the poorest child could enjoy bowling a hoop in the park or street. Wooden tops, too, cost very little in Victorian England, and included the small leather whip to keep them spinning.

THE MAGIC LANTERN  The first magic lanterns were children's toys, not adult entertainment. Victorian children were expected to learn through pleasure as much as possible. This new toy would certainly have thrilled them, even if it did not teach

them much! It was not a completely new idea to project pictures on to a screen for several people to see at the same time but it became popular in the nineteenth century. The slides or transparencies were hand-painted and beautifully produced.

**WHEELS AND MOVEMENT** Children have always loved small working versions of real vehicles such as carts and barrows. Railways were built from the 1820s onwards and toy railways soon followed. Victorian boys must have been thrilled by the miniature tin engines on sale. Some were working steam engines with real smoke. There were steam boats as well. But some of these toys were quite dangerous. If you know E Nesbit's story *The Railway Children* you will remember that Peter's engine exploded!

**BUTTONS, RIBBONS AND LACE** This carved wooden doll is dressed as a *pedlar* woman. Victorians loved anything in miniature. All the tiny objects in the doll's bag have been copied exactly from real ones. Her clothes are interesting because they show what the poorest people wore. The black housewife doll is really a bottle cover. Sometimes dolls were made without legs. They had a white face at one end of their bodies and a black one with turban and earrings at the other! Black boy dolls were popular too. Especially the smart golliwog with his bow tie.

FASHIONABLE DOLLS   Some of the beautifully-dressed dolls which survive from Victorian times are really fashion models or "Pandoras". Dressmakers made tiny complete sets of clothes—even underwear and stockings—in the latest fashions. They fitted the clothes on lovely wax dolls and sent them to customers or shops. This was cheaper than sending full-scale clothes. But if you look at the carefully-stitched tiny garments, it is difficult to believe it was any easier! Some lucky little girl would receive the clothes when they were out of fashion. I hope Anne Garlick got the wardrobe she wanted for her doll!

CLOCKWORK TOYS   Many Victorian toys worked by clockwork and were made of tin. There were beetles that flapped their wings, dancing monkeys, carriages, dolls and many other moving toys available quite cheaply—thanks to the use of tin in the 1880s. Metal toys had been made in Germany since the eighteenth century, but these were expensive. In Victorian times, street sellers sold cheap clockwork toys that many children could afford.

**THE YOUNG SHOPKEEPER** A simple game of shops would be great fun with the very fine butcher's shop seen here. It is fully equipped with removeable joints of meat. The idea was to teach little girls how to choose meat and how to weigh. This shop is English. The well-produced German shops sold in England at this time usually included a jolly butcher or grocer too! Shops like this were just as popular as dolls' houses in Victorian nurseries.

PENNY PLAIN   Victorian children had no television, of course, but they enjoyed making their own theatres. Pollock's toy theatres were the most famous of these cardboard cut-outs. The rather bloodthirsty plays, such as *Murder in the Wine Cellar*, satisfied their need for excitement! Originally, toy theatres were printed in pantomime programmes and cut out after a visit. But by the 1850s Pollock's were making full-scale plays with words, characters and scenery. These were beautifully designed—some ready-painted, and some plain for children to decorate themselves.

63

# 5. Toys From Other Lands

Have you ever wondered whether children in other countries enjoy toys like yours? Or how different their toys could be? Robert Louis Stevenson, remembering his own well-stocked Victorian nursery, asked:

"Little Indian Sioux or Crow
Little frosty Eskimo
Little Turk or Japanee
O don't you wish that you were me?"

The "frosty Eskimo" would have been playing happily with simple toys beautifully carved in wood or ivory. The children of Japan played with traditional kites and dolls. (But nowadays Japanese toys of every kind are sold in many countries. You probably have some, too.)

As we have seen, some toys are known the world over and have been played with since the earliest times. The Greeks knew about hoops. The Romans played with fivestones. The simple top and whip has been popular in Africa for centuries. And of course there must always have been dolls in every country.

In the Middle Ages, German wood-carvers made toys, especially dolls, to sell to other countries. So did Dutch craftsmen. A hundred years ago French dolls which could walk, talk and dance delighted rich children in many lands. And in this century, Russians have begun selling their nesting dolls abroad.

Nowadays, we are fortunate that we can share so many toys from all over the world.

DOLLS IN AMERICA   These British dolls are called Lord and Lady Clapham. Early settlers took dolls like this to America in the 1600s. "Apple Annie" dolls, made out of ordinary apples, were popular in the early 1900s. They were made in Montana, USA, by a mother and her daughter. First they dried the apples, then they painted and varnished them, and put in beads for eyes. The hands were apple slices, and the bodies wire and cloth. The dolls were dressed fashionably, or as mountain folk or Indian squaws. Now, a British woman makes apple-face dolls to resemble famous people, like the Queen.

RED INDIAN TOYS   North American Indians are famous for carving, and for creating beautiful objects in wood, leather, fur or beads. They made small animals in wood, sometimes covered in deer hide, for their children. Boys had miniature bows and arrows too. Girls strapped their "papooses" to

their backs! When explorers came to North America they brought toys and tiny articles to *barter* with the Red Indians. One voyager in 1585 took "glasses, knives and babies" (i.e. dolls). This little girl's doll is clearly from England! Notice the stiff Elizabethan style of the doll's clothing. Compare it with the girl's own primitive outfit.

DRAWING THE LINE IN MISSISSIPPI

**TEDDY'S BEAR** The teddy bear as we know it began life in America in 1903. President Theodore ("Teddy") Roosevelt refused to shoot a small bear cub when out hunting. You can see a newspaper cartoon of the story. A toy manufacturer asked permission to make a small bear and call it Teddy after the President. The toy was an instant success. Many famous people treasure their childhood bears. Perhaps you still have yours!

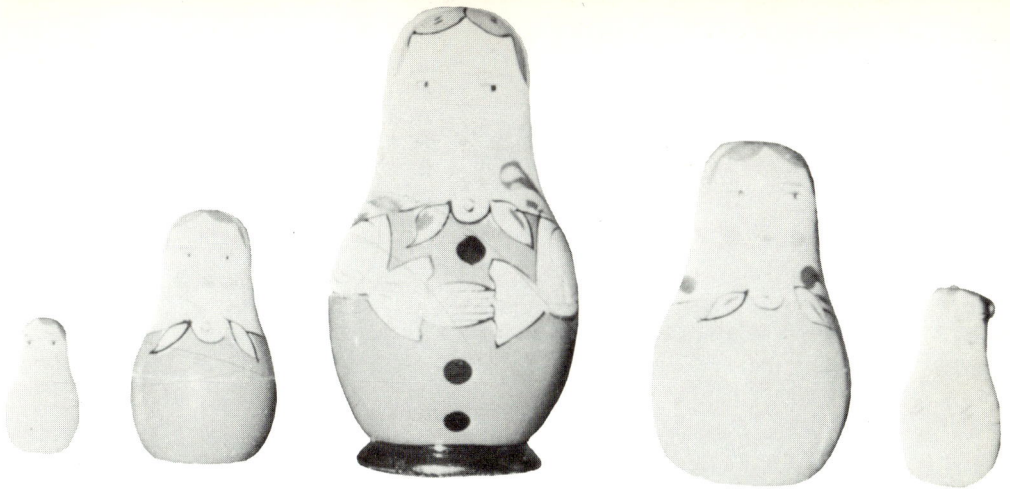

**RUSSIAN NESTING DOLLS** These fascinating, brightly-painted wooden dolls have been popular with Russian children since before 1850. They are usually called "babushka", which is Russian for "granny". The dolls nest one inside the next, according to size. They are interesting to play with, and educational, too. They train young eyes in grading size and order. And tiny fingers in screwing and unscrewing the joins in the middle of each doll. The wooden toys in the other pictures come from Russia and Denmark. The strings make the birds peck and the bears play.

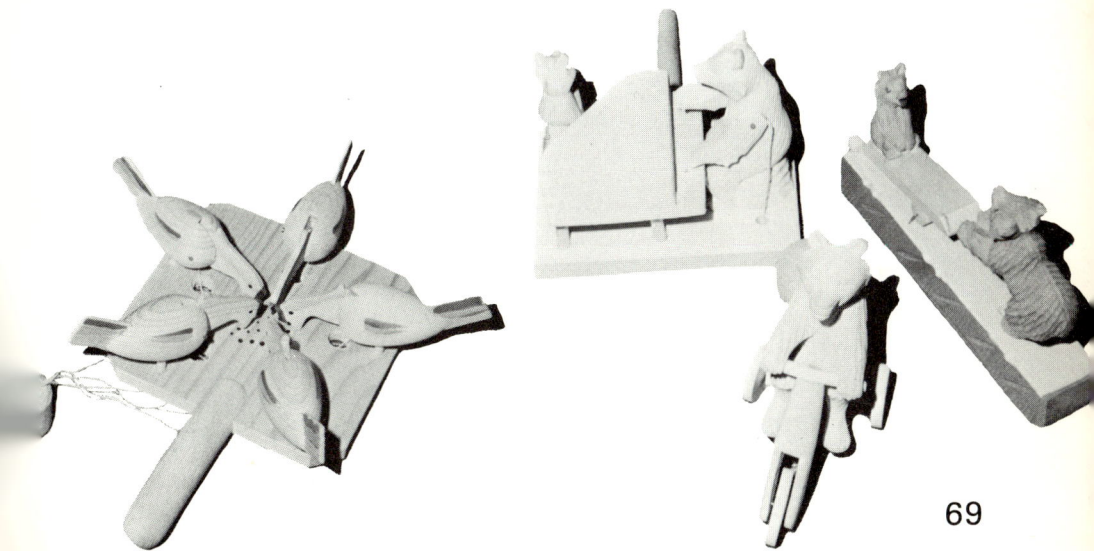

NATIONAL DOLLS   No doubt you know of a collection of dolls in interesting foreign costumes like this one. France alone has many different costumes. The dashing Spanish dancer in his attractive outfit would make a bright souvenir for a boy. Further afield, eastern dress is very different from European. There is a distinctive *oriental* look about some of these dolls.

BEAUTIFUL FRENCH DOLLS   The nineteenth century was the great age of beautiful, lifelike dolls. Many of these were made in France. The most famous dollmaker was Jumeau. His factory was in Paris. The dolls' bodies were made of soft leather. Their heads were modelled in wax and the eyes were glass. Each hair and eyelash was put in separately! Naturally, this kind of craftsmanship was expensive. Even in 1882 a French doll cost more than five pounds. But some of them could "talk" as early as 1880. Walking dolls were made earlier still.

**JAPANESE DOLL FESTIVALS** Dolls have a special significance for Japanese girls. So important are they, that there is a special festival on 3rd March when the dolls are carefully displayed. Often they are very valuable, having been handed down over many generations. They are never really played with. Little Japanese girls learn the complicated rituals of their tea ceremonies through moving their dolls into certain positions. The emperor is always in the most important place.

**GERMAN MECHANICAL TOYS** Germany has long been the home of fascinating moving toys, usually worked by clockwork. These *automata* were originally made by the clockmakers, as you might guess. Early clocks often had moving figures. Soon these dolls were made to dance and move independently of clocks. The German town of Nuremberg was so proud of its toymakers that it once forbade toys made anywhere else to be sold in the city!

EASTERN SHADOW PUPPETS  A very unusual kind of shadow play can still be seen in Indonesia today. The puppets are curiously-shaped flat figures called Wayangs. They are made of thin leather, bamboo or even paper, and their spiky limbs are operated by sticks. This kind of theatre, where only shadows are seen, has very ancient origins. The plays are mostly historical, to teach young people about their country's ways.

SWISS MUSIC BOXES  The charming tinkling sound of the music box is produced by little metal "teeth" on a rotating drum. Switzerland is the home of these delightful wind-up toys. Even today you can buy many different kinds. Tiny *chalets* are as popular as ever. But now jewellery boxes with turning ballerinas are often bought too. The Victorian music boxes which our great-grandmothers loved were usually bigger and heavier, with glass lids.

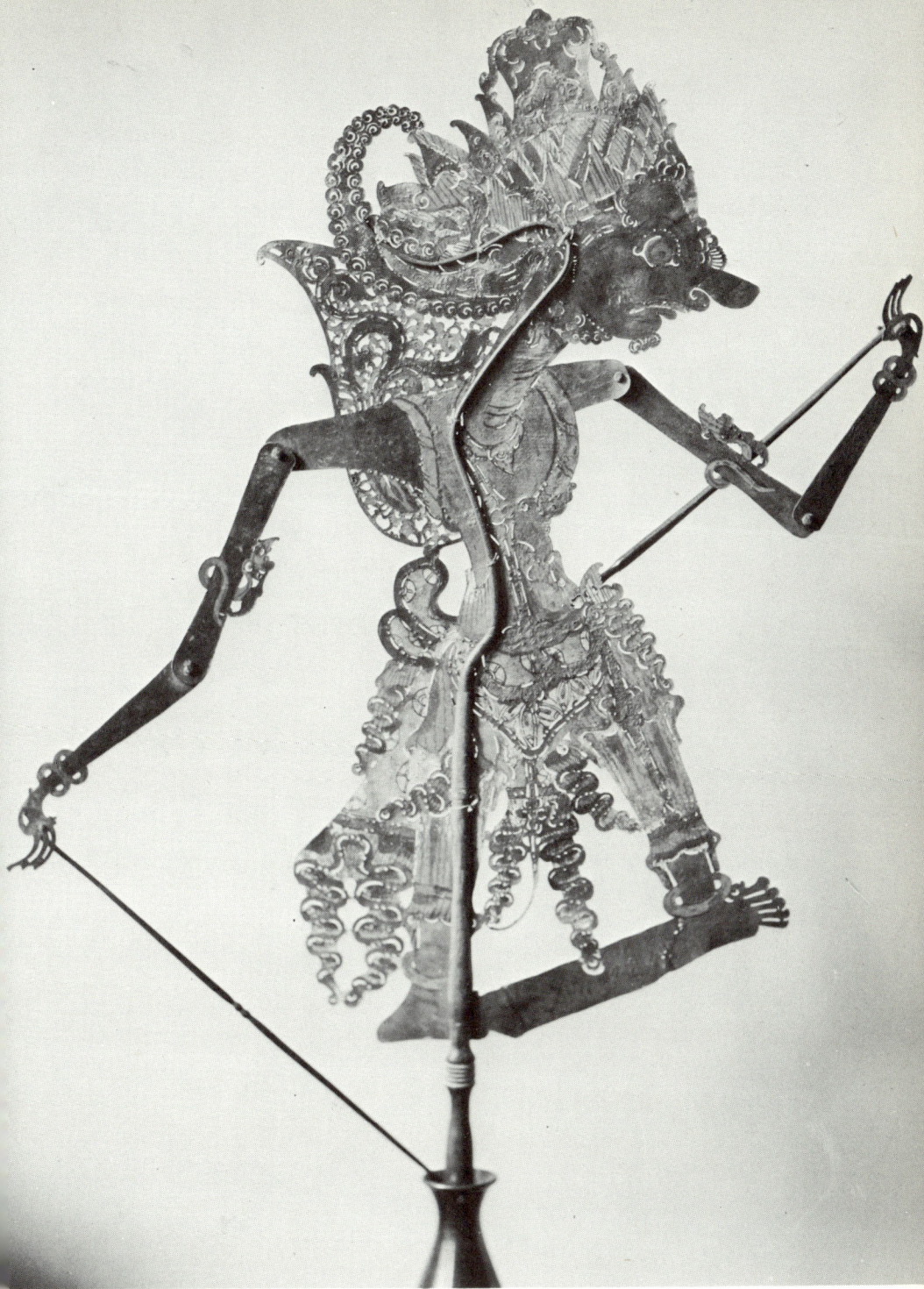

# 6. A Modern Wonderland

Today's toys are more wonderful than ever before. Modern techniques have given us remote-controlled helicopters, boats and even robots. Lights flash, model soldiers shout commands and dolls try to pour out tea! But many of these complicated amusements are more suitable for adults! For this reason the complicated *automata* of earlier chapters have come to rest almost unused in museums. These toys were never really loved and played with. Modern mechanical toys, too, are soon broken or discarded for simpler playthings with more scope for imagination. A doll with a hollow back for its recorded voice is less cuddly than a battered rag doll. And battery-driven marvels are soon worn out! Still, there is a wider choice of high-quality toys in the 1970s, particularly for outdoor play.

Many of the old-established toys are still popular, however. Some toys are actually *reproductions* of Victorian or Edwardian playthings. War toys, dolls of course, balls and wheeled vehicles have been enjoyed through the centuries. And they are just as popular today.

Even if modern babies play with rattles of plastic instead of coral, and balls of rubber instead of rag, the aim is the same as ever—to develop skills of mind and body ready for the adult world.

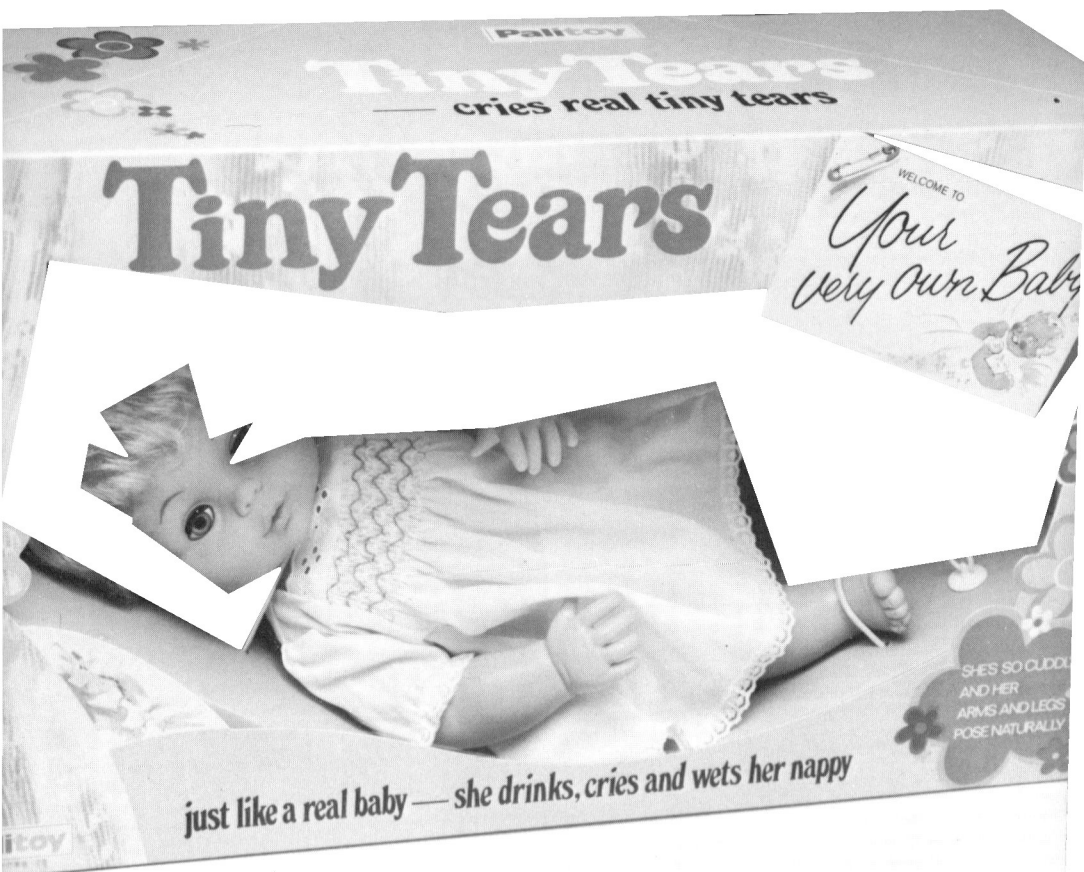

Palitoy

Tiny Tears — cries real tiny tears

Tiny Tears

WELCOME TO
Your very own Baby

SHE'S SO CUDDLY
AND HER
ARMS AND LEGS
POSE NATURALLY

just like a real baby — she drinks, cries and wets her nappy

Palitoy

DOLLS    Dolls are as popular today as ever they have been. A lifelike baby doll which drinks and wets has won a "Toy of the Year" award for several years. Other dolls walk with dogs, copy words at a desk or talk and sing. Modern "teenage" dolls have all manner of outfits and accessories to collect —even a boyfriend! Soft-bodied dolls often look old-fashioned and home-made.

**DOLLS FOR BOYS** Dolls are even made especially for boys now! The lead soldiers of the last century have been replaced by larger models. They have various detailed uniforms, tiny hand grenades and binoculars. For these Action Men there are magnificent jeeps, tanks and a hang-gliding kit. An offshoot of Action Man is the Six Million Dollar Man, complete with "bionic" eye and removable "bionic" works.

OUTDOOR PLAY    Most outdoor toys are shared in playgrounds. Adventure playgrounds have many exciting variations on swings, climbing frames and ladders. Children with gardens can play just as well

with home-made outdoor toys. A tree house needs very little apart from imagination. And a cast-off rubber tyre firmly fixed to a tree makes a super swing.

CRAZES   Crazes are nothing new. Fashions in toys, or a toy that just "catches on" across a country or over half the world, have been known for centuries. A few years ago the humble hoop took on new life as an exercise toy. It needed plenty of skill to keep it turning around the hips like a "hula" dancer! Yo-yos took the Western world by storm in the 1920s. More recently, a noisy toy called "clackers" was played with by nearly everyone. And I expect you and your friends have plastic kites!

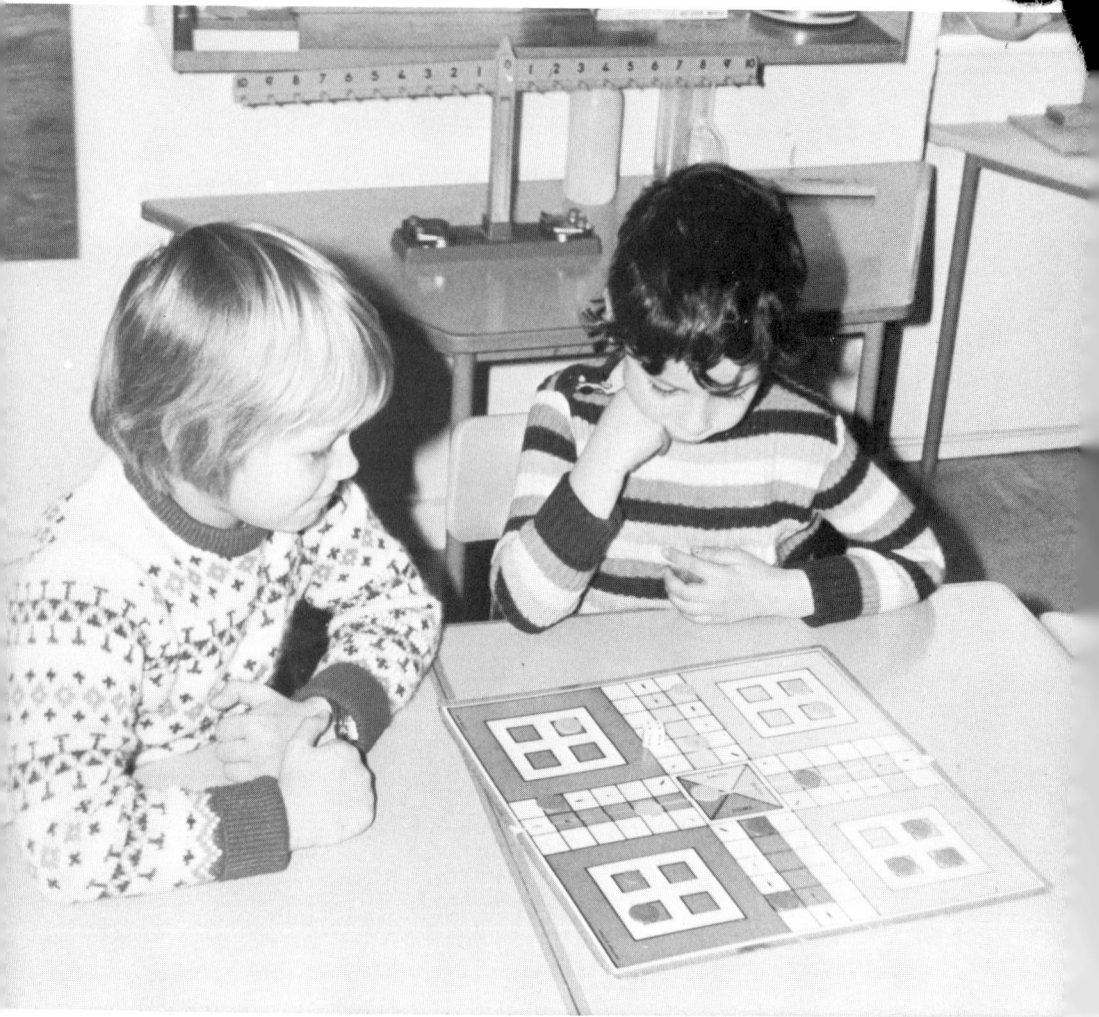

**BOARD GAMES**   Today's new board games seem very complicated, with many pieces to lose or break. Basically, the idea of chasing counters round a board by scoring with dice is still the same. But plastic mice and fighting robots are often included in today's boxes, too! Monopoly and the even older ludo (just the Latin word for "I play") are still bought in huge numbers at Christmas. Other older games such as backgammon are coming back into fashion for adults and children.

**PLAYING HOUSE** This simple, well-designed dolls' house is very different from earlier miniature houses. It has a collapsible framework of natural wood instead of a complicated structure. The idea is to leave as much as possible to the imagination. Lighting, wallpaper and even realism have been replaced by strength and simplicity. And this may be the most modern trend of all.

**MAKE BELIEVE**   Children have always wanted to dress up in their play, especially in grown-ups' clothes. Young people today are not limited to mother's cast-off shoes or the old net curtains. Toymakers produce detailed, small-size costumes for brides, astronauts, soldiers, policemen and even a Queen! Cowboy and Indian costumes, and nurses' uniforms are the most popular.

**KITS**   One of the most recent toys is the craft kit for making jewellery, pottery or plaster models. There are also kits for making models of the latest ships and planes. In the 1920s children were able to astound their friends with a box of conjuring tricks, or perform simple chemistry experiments with a kit. How amazed they would be at the possibility of sculpting, or embedding coins in transparent plastic today!

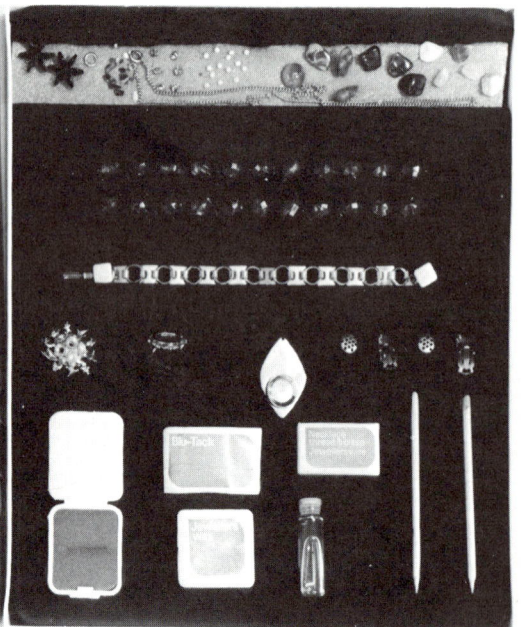

**ON THE MOVE** Wheeled toys have been popular since Roman times. Bicycles, pedal cars and "sit and ride" trains with carriages are just a few of the larger wheeled toys available today. There are lots of small vehicles too. Cars from all lands, tractors, fire engines, police cars and ambulances are popular modern miniatures. Many children buy them with their pocket money and collect whole sets.

RAL 00I

CONSTRUCTION AND BUILDING Building toys are not entirely modern. We saw alphabet bricks as early as Elizabeth I's time. But well-designed plastic bricks which fix together, like Lego, are an improvement. Lego was invented by a Dane called Oleg Christiansen in the 1950s. He used the letters of "Oleg" to make the name "Lego". Meccano, with its nuts, bolts and spanners, is slightly more complicated.

**PUPPETS** Puppets, as we have seen, are ancient and world-wide toys. They are no less popular today. Some are the kind of *marionette* which appeared in puppet shows in eighteenth-century Italy. Hand puppets are much easier to operate. They are often inspired by characters on children's television. Other toys, too, owe their popularity to television. Paddington Bear and the Wombles are cuddly creatures. Not the Daleks, though! There is a whole range of Dalek toys from pencil sharpeners to full-scale dressing-up outfits!

# New Words

| | |
|---|---|
| *Archaeologists* | People who seek facts about the ancient past |
| *Automata* | Toys which move automatically or when wound up |
| *Barter* | Exchange of goods for other goods, instead of for money |
| *Bobbin* | Wooden reel used in weaving and spinning |
| *Booth* | Portable canvas-covered framework for shows and stalls |
| *Chalet* | Little Swiss house, usually made of wood |
| *Dappled* | Spotted, especially used about grey and white horses |
| *Hadrian's Wall* | Defensive wall in northern Britain built by Emperor Hadrian in 130 AD |
| *Harpsichord* | Instrument which looks like a small piano with two keyboards. It sounds different from a piano because the strings are plucked and not struck by hammers |
| *Jute* | Strong thread for making ropes and mats. It comes from plants grown in Asian countries like Pakistan |
| *Jousting* | Mock fighting between knights on horseback |
| *Marionettes* | Jointed puppets worked by pulling strings |
| *Medieval times or Middle Ages* | Period between 1066 and 1500 AD |
| *Neolithic period* | New Stone Age, from about 3000–1800 BC in Europe. The |

|              |                                                        |
|--------------|--------------------------------------------------------|
|              | time when people started growing crops, keeping animals, weaving and making pots |
| *Ocarina*    | Small egg-shaped china instrument, blown by mouth      |
| *Oriental*   | From eastern countries, like China or Japan            |
| *Papyrus*    | Egyptian water plant used to make paper                |
| *Pedlar*     | Trinket seller who travelled the roads                 |
| *Reproduction* | Modern copy of something old                         |
| *Sash cord*  | Cord supporting windows which slide up and down        |

# Table of Dates

*Before Christ's birth*

| 2000 BC   | Egyptians make dolls and toys   |
|-----------|---------------------------------|
| *c.* 400  | Wheeled toys appear in Greece   |
| *c.* 200  | Kites used in China             |

*After Christ's birth*

| *c.* 900 AD | Vikings are playing chess            |
|-------------|--------------------------------------|
| 1100        | Pierotti family make dolls in Italy  |
| 1491        | Nuremberg toymakers form guilds      |
| 1825        | Dolls first made with eyes that close|
| 1836        | Walking dolls made in Paris          |
| 1895        | Golliwogs appear                     |
| 1901        | Meccano invented                     |
| 1903        | Teddy bears first made in America    |
| 1905        | The first toy aeroplanes             |
| 1950        | Lego marketed in Denmark             |
| 1970        | Action Man comes on the scene        |

# More Books

*A History of Toys* by Antonia Fraser (Hamlyn Spring Books, 1972). A big, beautifully-illustrated history covering a wide period. It is now out of print but you may find it in a library.

*A Victorian Sunday* by Jill Hughes (Wayland, 1972). Another book in this series. It gives an all-round picture of life in Victorian times, including toys and games.

*All Colour Book of Dolls* by Kay Desmonde (Octopus Books, 1974). Well-illustrated with large photographs of Victorian dolls.

*Dolls* by Antonia Fraser (Octopus Books, 1973). Another well-illustrated book. It is now out of print but may be in your local library.

*Dolls and Dolls' Houses* by Roger Baker (Orbis, 1974). Mostly photographs with captions. It has a short introduction.

*Growing Up in the Middle Ages* by Penelope Davies (Wayland, 1972). Another book in this series which gives information on games and playthings.


# Places to Visit

Bethnal Green Museum, London
Edinburgh Museum of Childhood
Kirkstall Abbey Folk Museum, Leeds
Min Lewis Pram Museum, Somerset
Pollock's Toy Museum, London
Victoria and Albert Museum, London

# Index

# Picture Credits

The author and publishers wish to thank all those who have given permission for copyright illustrations on the following pages: The Mansell Collection, *Frontispiece*, 6, 9 *top*, 10, 11, 12 *top*, 21, 34, 55, 62, 63, 75; Mary Evans Picture Library, 9 *bottom*, 24, 32–33, 39, 53, 56–57, 58; The Trustees of the British Museum, 25; Bethnal Green Museum, 71; Victoria and Albert Museum, 66; Leicester Museum, 8, 15; Leeds City Art Gallery, 29; Gordon Fraser Gallery, 30; Nostell Priory and Lord St Oswald, 38; the remaining pictures are the property of the Wayland Picture Library. The author and publishers also wish to thank Mr C R Jayne for photographing many of the toys and Leeds Museum, Eva Mitchell, Mrs C Stead and Broadgate Infant School for allowing toys in their possession to be photographed. In addition, the following manufacturers supplied photographs: Mettoy Playcraft, 76, 81, 86; Raleigh, 87; Thomas Salter, 84; Galt, 85, 90; Lego, 88, 89; Gabrielle Designs, 91.